the Relation Ship

the Relation Ship

WRITTEN BY
LUTHER & BERNICE CANADA

The Relation Ship

Copyright © 2020 by Luther and Bernice Canada

Printed in the United States of America. No part of this publication may be used or reproduced, stored in a retrieval system, transmitted in any form or by any means-electronic, mechanical, photocopy, recording, or by any information storage and retrieval system, except for brief quotations in printed reviews, without the prior written permission of the publisher.

ISBN: 978-0-9995869-8-3

iSeebookz Publishing, Suite 300 Commerce Ave., Ste 137B LaGrange, GA 30241

Book cover: Cheryl Litton and Priscilla Sodeke
Interior design: Priscilla Sodeke
Editors: Yolanda Rowland and Emily Salisbury

Personal Memoirs

Minimal editing to maintain authentic integrity.

First Edition: 2020
10 9 8 7 6 5 4 3 2 1

All rights reserved.

PROLOGUE

Building a Ship for Two

Luther

Sailing the seas of love, fear, and commitment, I have always found enjoyment and excitement swimming in the ocean. The Atlantic Ocean is the most beautiful body of water, on this planet earth, even when it appears to be angry. The tides and winds produced waves 10 to 12 feet high, and to swim out into the oceans deep, ride on top of the waves back to shore, that was the fun part. I learned there are hidden dangers in the high tides and waves swimming without skill. The ocean water can result in the instant death of drowning. The only way to survive is never venturing to defy the current over the top; it is always too much water. I learned to swim under the waves to be safe and live to see another day.

I must say that I learned to swim in a small fish pond in Alabama where you would think swimming was safe. I lost several friends to drowning, but I never lost my passion for swimming. God has always been with me, and he is with me now. This everlasting current that pulls us in is nature's equivalent to love. How it draws us in... I see it is of God.

Bernice

When we get up in the morning, the first thing we

are grateful for is that we woke up together. We give thanks to God, we have our cup of coffee together every morning, and then we talk and enjoy each other.

The closer you get to God, the closer you get to each other. There is no end with God in the midst. The more Luther and I stay connected with God, the more He stays with us.

We would not have made 40 years of marriage, if we had not stopped, and slowed down to see what each other was talking about. Listening intently to my husband, even just over a cup of coffee, is the ship I'll sail on forever.

CARDS IN THESE MODERN TIMES...

For My Wife...

I am so happy and even happier that I have someone as special as you.
Someone who loves me as special as you.

To my Darling Wife

Love Eternal your husband,

LUTHER

01.26.06

The Relation Ship

The Former Years

Bernice

I was a single, independent woman of twenty-four years, working and living alone. One day, while cleaning my house and living a lonely life, I talked to God about how lonesome I was and that I was ready for a husband. I asked Him to bless me with one. I talked to God about the kind of husband I would like to have.

I didn't just want any man, but one that was kind and would treat me with respect. A husband that would love me for who I was at this time. I invited God into my life and allowed him to be my guide. Three years later...

Luther

I was in New York praying for a wife, and she was in Alabama praying for a husband. We did not know each other; we had never met, indicating an act of God. In the beginning, I knew she was the God-sent woman to be my wife. There was no reason for me to doubt. I knew God had answered my prayers.

After many years of living single in New York, dating different women that did not reach my heart, I did some serious thinking: what was I missing from all my relationships? I could not understand why I felt unfulfilled? Life had to be more than work, as a commercial truck driver, only meeting people in 5 boroughs of New York City. What was evading me in life? What was the missing part, that needed to be found?

I made a decision. I needed to be married, thus ending the life of different relationships. I wanted a relationship where I was committed to one person forever. All I had to do was find the woman who I thought I could be happy with, but one that was not from New York, so my journey took me home to Alabama.

Bernice

I met this interesting man in the town where I lived. I was with my Aunt Lila, who knew him before he left and went to New York. I asked my Aunt Lila, who was the man that she spoke to and seemed to know very well. She told me his name was Luther. He made his presence known; he walked over to our car and said that he was visiting his mother for the summer. My Aunt Lila and Luther talked, then he met my sister and me.

Luther

I saw the most beautiful black woman that I had ever seen in all my life. Instantly, I knew she could be my future happiness and there was no doubt in my mind that she was the woman that I wanted to marry and spend the rest of my life with.

Seeing her strengthened my decision to end-all of the other relationships. I was in awe and thought, *to have this beautiful black southern woman as my wife,* I knew I would be happy. Would she say yes to my question of marriage? Did I have a chance with her? We started talking that day. I wanted to see if we could begin a relationship before I had to return to my

Bernice

I invited him to my home, and during the conversation, he stated that he was busy looking for land to buy; he was having a house built for his mother. He let me know that he had to return to New York in a few days, but would try to stop by before he had to leave.

A few days had passed, and he came to visit me. We went out to lunch and we talked. He said he was looking for a wife, and that he would be back in a month on business for the house to be built. We talked, and he asked if I was dating anyone; I said I was not. He said he was not dating anyone either, and had been praying for a wife. Amazingly, I had been praying for a husband.

job in New York. She told me to come to her house before I left. This was the beginning of happiness for me.

Luther

I was happy and now I had a chance to introduce her to some of my ideas of dating. I wanted her to experience dating from a man that was years older and experienced. I wanted our dating life to be exciting and distinctive from any other men she may have dated.

So, I asked her if she could find the time for us to go on a date to Wind Creek State Park. She informed me that for the next two days, she was off from her job. That was wonderful news. I told her I would be there at ten o'clock in the morning to pick her up. She said that she would be waiting for me. I could feel the excitement in her voice, which gave me the confidence that I needed. I drove away happy. I felt that meeting her and the starting of this journey into a relationship was what I was missing from my life.

The next day when we arrived at Wind Creek State Park, I could see the look of amazement in her eyes. She looked around at all the beauty; she took in the colorful trees and the lakes of blue water with islands in the middle with tall trees. Thinking back, it looked like a painted picture. I could tell that she was happy on our first date, giving me the feeling that it would not be our last. We had a great time. My heart was telling me it was no longer just a relationship, but something more.

I only had a week before I needed to return to New York. I wanted to take her on one more date before I left. I kept thinking about The Varsity and Atlanta; I had spent some time working as a janitor at the Georgia Tech College. The Varsity, a restaurant, was close to Georgia Tech. When construction was finished, and it first opened for business, was an exciting time. The idea of having lunch there every day, especially with the chili dogs and their peach pies being the best in all of Georgia, was an exciting one.

I enjoyed my time with her and the traditional southern menu of fast food with her. I was especially happy about our developing relationship and the seriousness of our connection.

Unfortunately, my visit to the south had come to an end, and I had to get back to my job in New York without further delay...

BERNICE

When he came back from New York, we started our relationship. He lived with his mother in Alabama until construction began on her house. Then, he went back to his job in New York. We kept the relationship close by Postal service and the telephone. The way our relationship was progressing forward, he showed patience. In his letters, he would let me know when he was going to call, like on Saturday evening for example.

He would say to me, "Make sure you are home."

LUTHER

There was no more extended time left for me to stay longer. The boss on my job told me he needed me back in New York. I had stayed in Alabama past the time that we had talked about before I left New York. I did have a good boss, and I left the next day going back to my job. After arriving back in the city, and starting back to work, I missed the new love in my life and the thought of her excited me.

She made me happy, and without a doubt, I knew I was in love with her. I wanted to marry her with a passion; I knew it was something that would make my life complete. I needed to do whatever to make it happen as soon as possible. There hadn't been a woman, that excited me more by just a thought. I wanted to be with her.

BERNICE

Luther and I made our long-distance relationship work. I received a letter from him every week and a phone call every Saturday or Sunday. It was clear that he cared for me. He was doing everything a man would do when he found the woman he wanted to marry. True love will make you listen to each other with respect because you want the relationship to last. If you have problems, sit down and talk about it to each other.

To my wife

This is my beloved and this is my friend
Song of Solomon 5:16

*Today, I celebrate our love.
I thank God for you and for the beauty of our Marriage.
All my love on Valentine's Day.*

Love, your husband,

Luther

02.14.06

Luther

Now that I was back in New York, and back on the job, I knew I had to stay busy. My work kept the lonely feelings from my everyday thoughts. When I thought of the precious times we had together, in Alabama, I missed her. I had a new love in my life and was thinking of marriage. I told my friends in New York, and to my surprise and amazement, not one of my friends thought I should get married, including my boss.

But to the contrary, I knew it was totally my decision and mine alone. Knowing God was with me and in me; he would also be in the marriage, with no reason to doubt it, it made me very happy. After talking to some of my friends, once I returned to New York, I wanted to bring some excitement back to my life. The first thought that came to my mind was Coney Island. Since living in New York, it was the most exciting area that I had ever visited. There was so much to see and do.

Bernice

We dated a year before we got married, and I prayed about our relationship. I prayed to God, asking Him to not let anything happen if Luther was not right for me. I knew I would be alright; the Lord was with me. Luther came back home one more time before we got married.

He took me to Atlanta, Georgia and bought my rings. I was so happy that he kept the relationship wonderful and I could depend on him. Whatever he said he would do, he kept his word. I could feel God, and within the relationship, He was with us all the way. I trusted God and He came through for us in a powerful way.

I kept praying and talking

to the Lord to be sure I was not making a mistake by doing the wrong thing with my life. I was willing to give him up if I had to, but the Lord guided me all the way with a good and happy feeling to the date of the marriage.

Luther

After the relationship had lasted over one year, I decided to go back to Alabama and seriously talk marriage with her. I wanted to get back to my love in Alabama. The summer season was starting soon, and the oil fuel business was slow in the summer. I knew it would be easier for me to talk to Mr. Fazio, my boss, for some time off, without him refusing. Mr. Fazio granted me a month off from work to return to Alabama.

He also added, "That girl is going to make you leave New York, and I will have to find another truck driver."

I told him, "No, I love New York too much to move back to the south."

Mr. Fazio replied, "Ok, just watch what I am telling you."

After Mr. Fazio said I could take the time off I needed to return to Alabama, I decided it was time to call Bernice. I wanted her to know that I was coming back to Alabama and I hoped that we could get married. But, I only wanted to if she still had the same love and desire she had for me at the beginning of our relationship. She said we would talk more in detail about the marriage when I returned to Alabama. That was enough positive confidence for me to make the trip south.

Bernice

We decided on June 2, 1979, to be the date for our wedding. On the day of our wedding, he was thirty-seven, and I was twenty-seven years of age.

My family liked him, even though they barely knew him. They recognized he was serious about me. Admiring his dedicated character and personality, they liked the way he carried himself within the relationship. His sincerity in how he treated me was something special to my family.

Luther

I left New York the next week, to avoid the heavy New Jersey turnpike traffic on the weekend. I had more than twenty years of experience driving from New York to Alabama. It was time for me to have a wife, and if this was to be a blessed trip, I would not have to continue driving twelve hundred miles alone, with no one to talk to. I was very pleased with that thought after arriving home in Alabama. I called Bernice to find out how soon could we talk. She said she didn't have to work the next day and we could spend the day making plans discussing the details of getting married. I did not know about weddings, but I let her talk. I listened to her and supported her financially in regards to the wedding.

Bernice

I kept praying and talking to the Lord, and he guided me all the way. I want to say to anyone reading, don't ever think He doesn't hear you when you talk or pray to Him sincerely. God will answer you. He answered me while I was living in Alabama, and Luther was living in New York. God connected us, and I was glad that I learned to pray for Luther. God heard me and He does answer prayers. All we have to do is believe and have faith in Him.

*Honest, Understanding,
Strong, Big-hearted, Affectionate,
Nurturing, Dependable.*

*I love you for all you are to me.
My life my love my everything.*

Happy Anniversary

*Darling, I love you
and please don't consider this
as a measurement of my love for you
because it is unmeasurable.*

Love you so much,

Luther

06.02.18

LUTHER

Arrangements and preparations became a reality; I was very happy they were no longer imaginary, and only in my mind. I could feel that this was the beginning of a New World for me. *I was anxious to step into this new world to manifest my life.* I knew only God himself could convince me that the marriage was blessed. I was ready to do whatever I had to do to have her for my wife with no exceptions.

The time had come for me to tell my mother. She had met Bernice once or twice, and that was concerning a business transaction with her while I was in New York. When I was sending money to my mother, I knew I could trust Bernice. She is the kind of woman to marry, and because marriage is built on trust, and love will always follow. Talking to my mother was never difficult. I could always talk to her about anything important in our lives.

It has always been my mother and me, with God taking care of both of us. I did not have my father in my life. I saw him one time. I remember it was during a time when school was starting back. He took me to town and bought me a pair of jeans, one flannel shirt, and he said he'd be back. I believed him, but he never came back and that disappointment only made me love my mother more, (without him).

When I told my mother that we were going to marry, she said, "That is what I have been waiting to hear you say. I believe she will be the best wife you could find. I know her people, and they are all good. Her Aunt Florence has been fixing my hair for a long time, and her Aunt Lila and I, always talk when we see each other in town. So, you have my blessings to marry into that good family."

I told my mother that her words made me very happy. Because we should feel the same way about who I brought into our family. I was and still am very much in love with her. I want to be the best husband that any woman could find, and to treat her with the respect she deserved.

Now that I had talked to my mother about the upcoming marriage, it was time to find out what day Bernice wanted to get married so that I could be back in New York, to keep Mr. Fazio happy with me. Mr. Fazio and I always had the best friendship that an employer and employee could have. But now, I was going to have a wife to take care of and support.

Bernice

Luther and I stayed close by keeping in contact with each other until he came home a week before the wedding; to prepare for the ceremony.

Luther

After I talked to Bernice, she let me know that she had decided on June the second to be the official wedding date. She asked if this was satisfactory with me, and gave me time to be back on my job in New York.

Bernice

The wedding was going to be at 4 o'clock pm on a Saturday, with Pastor Willie J. Brown officiating.

Luther

When I told her that she had my full cooperation, Bernice looked at me, giving me that beautiful smile she had when I first met her. It was a great mental feeling for me after talking with my mother, and learning she approved of the marriage. My mother's approval made it easier to continue thinking positive toward the wedding date with the woman that God had sent to be my wife. This decision, my decision was mine and mine alone; was without any interference. I just wanted to make my future wife and myself happy with God and HIS blessings always in the marriage.

Now it was my chance to talk to my best friend and ask him if he would be my best man. He happily accepted and congratulated me. He asked what time was the wedding, and I said at 4 o'clock. He said he would pick me up at my mother's house.

Happily, that completed my responsibility for all the important details I could think of to be expected of the groom. I rested my mind from all the anxiety I had experienced earlier; all the preparations that I thought the groom should be concerned about before the wedding. God was my support system. HE gave me strength and the knowledge that I did not have to worry about all of the small details. If there were any overlooked details, they would be too small to be noticed. I was extremely happy thinking of how I would soon be married to the most beautiful woman my eyes had ever seen.

It was 9 a.m. on the day of the wedding. It was a sunny and beautiful morning. I went out to the back yard so I could wash my car for the trip to Atlanta.

At exactly three-thirty, the evening of the wedding, Edward drove in front of my mother's house, blowing his car horn loudly, indicating his excitement. I was happy that his timing was perfect for our arrival at the church; it was a very short distance from my mother's home.

When we arrived at the church, all the parking spaces were filled. We went inside and sat in the back of the church to wait for the preacher; shortly, he came out into the sanctuary. Edward and I went to the front of the church for him to direct us on how he wanted us to stand. We wanted to be pleasing to God and proper before man. The preacher told us to stand with him.

My bride had not arrived.

When it became time for the wedding, we continued to stand in front of the sanctuary, with the church pastor. After a reasonable amount of time had passed, she walked in. She was more beautiful to me than I could have imagined possible for any bride to be presented to a groom. I could only think this was a marriage that would be everlasting to death. And with that thought, I was exceedingly happy.

After the bride arrived, the wedding vows were honored to make the marriage official, and we were pronounced Mr. and Mrs. Luther Canada. Since the first day, my eyes held a great feast, seeing her for the first time. This was the presentation I had been anticipating. The day she would be my wife. To have and to hold.

Bernice

It was a beautiful ceremony, with the Lord Supper included. After the wedding, we had a reception party that lasted into the evening with family and friends of the Bride and Groom.

We went to Atlanta, Georgia the next day for our honeymoon. We stayed in Atlanta, a few days, only to return to Alabama, and prepare for our trip to New York. We left Alabama traveling to New York as husband and wife.

We lived in Brooklyn after we got married. When he first brought me to New York, he introduced me to his friends. One of Luther's friends said, "You went to Alabama to get you a wife, with all of these women here in New York?"

I laughed about it, because I knew why his friend made the statement. His friends understood Luther, his kind, sweet, and caring ways. Plus, Luther knew what he wanted. What he was looking for, he didn't find it in New York.

He took me on an exciting adventure to Coney Island. There was so much to see and do. We had fun walking on the boardwalk in the hot sun, with the cool breeze blowing off the ocean. It made me extremely happy to be married and living in New York. He encouraged me to go on one of the rides called, "The Cyclone". I will never forget "The Cyclone", and I would never ride it again.

The ride ran on tracks like a freight train. It started very slowly, and then it climbed to one hundred feet above the ground, dropping suddenly, and then speed up to seventy-five miles per hour. It went around curves and on straight tracks. "The Cyclone" was too long for me. After the horrifying experience, Luther took me to Nathan's, a world-famous fast food place, to eat hot dogs, seafood, hamburgers, boiled corn, and french fries. It is one of the most sought after locations to eat on Coney Island.

We had fun eating and drinking cold beverages. We always enjoyed going to the West Indian Festival every Labor Day on Eastern Parkway at Prospect Park. When we moved back to Alabama, we continued to visit New York for several years to enjoy the fun and excitement of the festival.

Luther also took me to Aqueduct Race Track, where the horses raced daily on Rockaway Boulevard in South Ozone Park. Plus, there was a large flea market on the race track. It was nice. We traveled by subway transit system most of the time, to avoid looking for parking spaces for the car.

Sheep's Head Bay was another location where we enjoyed spending our time. It was on the ocean shore, and most of the residents were retired, senior citizens. We would have chosen the bay as our place to live, but we were too young. We often enjoyed taking our senior friends to lunch in the area. There were several nice restaurants to choose from with fresh seafood, which came in daily on ships. The fresh catch of the day would be from ships that left the docks early in the morning, going out to sea. They would fish all day and return to the dock at four in the evening.

Luther loved the water, and during our first year, he took me to the dock by the sea. Luther and I would wait for the ships to dock to purchase fresh fish. I love fresh fish. It was a treat to get bluefish, my favorite, along with shrimp and flounder. Sheep's Bay was a special place, and if I had the opportunity, I would visit again. I loved it.

We also enjoyed going to John Kennedy Airport, on some days, after supper to see the planes flying low over our heads to make a landing; I found it very exciting. He gave me a surprise birthday party, during my first year there, with a few friends. It was the best birthday party. We ate at Charlie's Restaurant and had entertainment in Long Island N.Y. He had something for us to do every weekend. One weekend he took me to see a movie with some friends. After the movie, we went to Manhattan for dinner. We also attended church regularly on Sundays.

LUTHER

After the wedding, we began the honeymoon of a lifetime for my lovely bride and me. The thought of advanced expectations was exceedingly exciting. It was what I needed to calm the anxiety I had experienced for several days. Could I be the man to make my bride the best husband that said the words *I do*? I was ready to take the challenge, and only time would tell the curious in mind. I hoped not to disappoint. We moved back to New York for me to continue work. I showed her Coney Island and all of my favorite spots in the city. I was the happiest man in New York.

BERNICE

We lived in NY for a few years, then his mother's health started failing, and we returned to Alabama.

After our return, Luther eventually moved his church home to where I was a member. He started to get involved and became very active in the church. I went back to work in nursing and my husband was hired to work in law enforcement. I was advised that he had to go to the Police Academy. He graduated and started working as a police officer. He worked as a police officer for several years until the Sheriff offered him a job to work with the Sheriff Department. He considered the offer a Promotion as he continued to work in law enforcement. Luther accepted the offer and started work as a Tallapoosa County Deputy Sheriff. He did a good job working for the Sheriff Department, the residents of Tallapoosa County, and was like throughout the county. His work with the Police Department combined with the Sheriff Department was a total of twenty years.

It was sufficient time for him to retire with God's blessings free of scandal or incident; resulting in a good, clean working record in law enforcement. We still continue to have a blessed marriage. God is good.

The Relation Ship

The Reality of Being a Co-Captain

∽

Before I met Luther, I had transportation, a job, and a home. I was a self-sufficient, independent woman. However, when I moved to New York, I wasn't working. I wanted to work, and I discussed it with Luther. His response,

"You don't have to work. I make enough money; I can take care of us. You will make me happy if you stayed at home, have my bath and dinner ready for when I come home."

I loved his words, for they meant he was looking forward to us spending the rest of our lives together.

I smiled at him and said, "I am just used to working Luther."

Being the man that I love, he stated, "If that's what you want, I have a friend whose wife works at a commercial printing corporation. It is located downtown Brooklyn under the Brooklyn Bridge. They print tags for major corporations."

I took Luther's suggestion. The work was interesting, and one day I came home and told my husband I did not want to go back. He asked what had happened and I explained to him the men always used profanity. Luther said I did not have to go back, and I became a housewife.

We had a savings account at East New York Savings bank, and we were able to do well together without me working.

One day, not long after we were married, Luther came home from work, and I cooked peas, okra, squash, and meatloaf with cornbread.

He said, "All the food smells so good to me. I could smell the food as I came inside the apartment." Luther told me that after coming home, the surprise was on him. He thought he was going to have to do everything, including the cooking. He wanted me for his wife, and he had no reservation with expected wifely duties.

The Relation Ship

Staying Afloat when the Honey Moon Ends

∽

I have learned in marriage to be concerned for each other in a spiritual, mental, and healthy way. To have a conservative thought when relating to expenses of the household, such as: utilities, fuel for vehicles, diet, on-time payments, and insurance premiums to avoiding late charges or cancellations.

When Luther and I worked, we never had a conflict concerning our finances during our forty years of marriage. When we took vacations, we always remained conscious of our spending; we considered the cost of food and beverages. However, we choose to only stay at quality hotels for cleanliness and safety. We were always concerned about keeping bills current. When we returned home, Luther was concerned in regards to my needs, as I was for his; whether it related to shoes, clothes, and other accessories we needed.

We work together cohesively. He loves to know what I am listening to, and if I am paying attention to events in the world, like the latest news or the weather locally and globally. Our marriage has made me wiser; I was only used to doing for myself without asking anyone for help.

God has truly blessed our marriage. If we have a problem, we work it out together. Prayer is a part of our everyday life. We put our trust in God to make our marriage work and to keep it strong. So, we communicate, no matter what it is.

Our relationship and faith in God are important to us. When you have a sincere, personal relationship with God, He will help and manifest Himself in your life and marriage. Luther and I have been blessed for forty years. Our happiness now is just as wonderful as it was the first day we got married. I can honestly say nothing has changed except we love each other more. Keep God first and ask HIM to do it for you.

Marriage is the foundation of society, and of civilization itself. God's primary purpose for a couple is to be happily married if they want it to work. Inviting God into your life is the key to getting to know Him. If you or your spouse are not affiliated with a church, find one and start attending. The church gives you the guidance and the foundation to learn more.

God knew with Him in the midst, two souls sharing life together would discover and learn the richness and the joys of marriage. The sanctity of the married couple is bound together. It is spoken of as a covenant, a term used for the most solemn binding agreement.

The Relation Ship

Sailing into the Horizon

☙

Presently, Luther and I are both retired, and we spend a generous amount of our time together doing missionary work. We do what we can as often as we can, visiting the sick and those stationed at home. We stay focused on our mission work. It is our first priority to be available when we are needed.

Luther and I also have a card ministry for our families, for their birthdays. We also select people to add to our list that are not family. This ministry is our way of showing love by reaching out to others and touching lives.

We wake up each morning talking, as this is our way of finding out and showing concern for each other's well-being. We like to take walks in the mornings and try to eat as healthy as we can, with fruits, vegetables, oatmeal, fish and drinking plenty of water. We try to stay stress-free by taking naps after lunch. We strive daily to do all these things to maintain a healthy lifestyle.

We enjoy our time together, but as we get older, we sometimes wish we could have had children. I think about it more these days. It is a conversation that we have with God. It is the one aspect of our life that is missed. However, Luther and I tell each other that God only wanted us to be happy together, and in the absence of children.

Sometimes we are like children. I remember the Christmas of 2018 when Luther cooked steaks on the grill. It had been several years of not cooking on Christmas, and the meal was delicious. It was a joyful occasion. During our time together over the years, we have become older, and yet we have also grown closer. We love each other more today than we did when we first said I do. It is a blessing, only because we've always keep GOD first.

We don't travel as we did in our earlier years. However, Luther is still able to take me wherever I want to go. My husband has done the grocery shopping for us. He does a great job, even if I am not with him. If we need anything that I think is special, I let him know. Luther is a tremendous help around the home as well. There are two country stores, a few miles from us. They sell all kinds of country food. We try to wake up early on Thursday and visit the stores.

When I first met Luther, he was wearing all western gear. He looked great in the boots, hat, jeans, jacket, belt, and all the accessories of an urban cowboy from New York. He looked and acted like a man who knew where he was going in life. He is the kind of man that I can talk to, no matter what, and that keeps us happy. We talk about married life regularly and who joined us together. We stay in prayer daily.

Praying to God to bless you for things that you want him to do in your life is important, because only He can make it unique for you. Through prayer, my marriage is a blessing. Praying every day with my husband, I feel special. He himself makes me feel special. I can still remember when I lost my wedding band; it was a beautiful band and special to me. I let Luther know that I had lost it.

He saw that I was hurt about it, and he told me, "I will get you another one when I can."

He got me another one just like the ring I lost. Our birthdays are close, only a month apart. On my birthday, we have cake and ice cream. However, we celebrate both of our birthdays on Luther's, by going out on a special date.

I remember on a weekend shopping trip to Atlanta, after buying a few things at the mall, I noticed a beautiful dress for ninety-nine dollars. On our return trip to Alabama, I told Luther about it. He stated I should have said something at the time.

The next day while I was sleeping, and without my knowledge, he went to Atlanta and bought it. When I woke up, he showed me the dress. When I told Luther where to find the dress, and what it cost, I didn't mean for him to get the dress without me. But I was so happy. That is the kind of husband that I married. There is not anything too big or too small that we wouldn't do for each other.

JOINT EPILOGUE

After four decades of marriage and counting, I am still praying to God for a long, healthy, spirit-filled life with Luther.

There is not anything too big or small that we wouldn't do for each other. God keeps his word. Although that does not guarantee a husband and wife won't go through difficult things in married life. First, you learn to care about each other, respect boundaries, work together, and then love grows. I can't say it enough, the importance of having a relationship with God and always put Him first should be inherent.

Occasionally, young ladies ask for my advice concerning their love interest. One young lady who was in a relationship for the second time with a man she loved, was worried about the children from a previous marriage. I told her to pray about it and let God fix it. I told her this might not be the one and not to worry — God makes no mistakes.

I tell Luther often that we are one of the happiest couples in the world, simply because of our communication with God. Every day, Luther and I pray to God and tell HIM what's on our mind, especially if we are having problems. We put them on the table for God to handle, with the understanding that God can handle everything, even when we can't. I am so glad God let me and Luther live together as husband and wife, four decades and counting.

What therefore God hath joined together, let not man put asunder.

MARK 10:9 KJV

ABOUT THE AUTHORS

Luther and Bernice Canada are native residents of Alabama. They are a God-fearing couple who have dedicated their lives to service. Luther Canada is a retired sheriff deputy, and Bernice Canada is a retired assistant health care provider. On a good day, you will find them visiting the sick and shut-in, preparing meals for those less fortunate, and enjoying their card ministry where they send cards to endearing family and friends for birthdays and special occasions. The Relation Ship is their first publication. Their mission in writing is to give insight and to bring awareness that married life as God has ordained is still viable in this modern age.

EDITORS THOUGHTS

∽

It is beautiful to read about a simple yet pure love of two individuals that look beyond faults and see the person for who they are; and seeing two individuals working toward a common goal.

Luther and Bernice are living a life filled with love and understanding. Their life requires being honest with self. Knowing who you are and what you want and not settling; to embrace a higher plane of thought beyond blame, to be honest, and to operate in integrity at all times. Not because it is required, but because it is a part of your character, and you see your partner as an extension of yourself. Thus, you wish no harm, and you love unconditionally, working to make the best of what is given, as an individual, and collectively for the relationship.

As a society, we look for the easiest, and the fastest route, not realizing the best things in life, takes time to be developed and cultivated. Thus, its value becomes precious. Luther and Bernice represent a beautiful relationship, a diamond shining, but they didn't start as a diamond.

They endured singlehood and the issues that came with it, until they individually realized, I want something more in life. They always thought of marriage, but it wasn't until they were truly seeking it, and wanting it did they find each other. Their story talks briefly of their struggle in singlehood. It sheds a little light on the pressure of living alone and wanting more.

It showed patience and waiting for the right one, the one that would cultivate the best in them as a couple and as individuals.

They didn't settle for cubic zirconia, which only takes weeks for development into its full form. They wanted a diamond relationship, one only that the divine Maker of all Things could create.

How long does it take to make a diamond? Well, according to Google search, it's not a fast process, nor is it easy. A diamond forms in the earth's mantle in extreme temperatures and is delivered to the earth surfaced by a volcanic eruption.

Bear in mind the entire diamond process takes between 1 billion and 3.3 billion years, which is a quarter to three-fourths of the earth's total age, and it's developed under immense pressure and extreme temperatures. A relationship will have its problems, but are you willing to be a diamond couple? Are you looking to be cubic zirconia or just sand upon the beach washing away with the tide?

Many people choose to be in a relationship. However, are they willing to become a diamond?

Have they taken the time to realize it takes work? Did they consider divorce as a non-option? Did they take inventory on themselves; what do I have to offer that would make the other person better by being with me? Do you have a partner who is willing and dedicated to withstand the years passing by, looking back and saying 16, 39, 45, or 61 years married? Ultimately, saying until death do us part, and never regretting the day they said I DO. All of the above questions are important. And the answers validate the commitment of being true to one's self in order to sustain what God has joined together let no one put asunder. 🌱